The Adventures of Samuel Bear

Betty Salthouse

With illustrations by

Holly Salthouse

THE ADVENTURES OF SAMUEL BEAR

Published by Hawkesbury Press 2021
www.hawkesburypress.com

ISBN 978-1-911223-79-5

Illustrations by Holly Salthouse
Interior design by Debbie Young
Edited and proofread by Dan Gooding

This book is dedicated to bears everywhere,
who share our planet with us,
inspiring our stories and literature,
and to my granddaughter Holly,
who illustrated it

1

Splodge Leaves the Zoo

Bertha Bear wanted something better for her cub: independence! So when he was old enough, she pushed him between two loose bars of their cage at the zoo.

But not without a tear in her eye. He was particularly special, the only cub she'd produced in 15 long years. The zoo vet had named him Splodge after seeing little more than a smeary speck on a television screen, showing a new life.

"Think of me, and I'll be there," Bertha called to her precious child, as Splodge scampered away, just before the keeper arrived with his heavily laden food trolley.

"Morning Apricot," said Mr Tidy the keeper, because Bertha's brown coat had apricot tints. "Got something special for you today."

He lifted up a big bunch of bananas.

True, bananas were her favourite, but she would rather have picked them herself.

As she ambled towards them, Bertha tried not to think of Splodge. While Bertha was busy eating, Mr Tidy had the chance to peek inside her cage. He was always careful, because mothers of small infants can be extremely tetchy.

But of Splodge there was no sign.

Meanwhile, Splodge had done as he was told. Following his mother's push and her cry of "GO!", he'd squ-ee-zed out. But what had she meant when she said "Make a life for yourself"? What was a life? All he'd known was the square space he'd shared with his mother's warm body, and the humans who came in all shapes and sizes to stare at him.

"You must learn to live like humans and behave like humans," Bertha had told him once, pointing at a particularly happy-looking character with a duffle coat and warm scarf. So clever Splodge quickly found a cart and rode out of the zoo, hidden beneath a smelly load of rubbish.

Outside he discovered that humans had cages too, but they were made of bricks, and they could come and go as they pleased. He watched them at a safe distance.

It wasn't long before the newspapers were full of "Missing Bear Cub" reports. Meanwhile he sneaked milk from doorstop bottles and cleared up the remains outside the greengrocers' shops, and he managed to get by.

Then, early one bright morning, when the salty air was wafting up from the river, a friendly rat told him, "What you want is a place in the country."

So Splodge headed out of town. Luckily, one fine day, he found himself in the garden of some explorers, at Honeysuckle Cottage in Windy Wood.

The explorers were the weirdest pair, with wrinkled skin from the heat of many expeditions, but with lively spirits and generous hearts.

"Look what we've got here," said one.

"The escaped bear cub!" said the other.

They had read all about it in the newspaper.

"But we won't turn him in," they said. "He can live with us."

2

A Surprise in the Forest

So that's how little Splodge grew up to be Mr Samuel Beresford Bear. A well-educated bear who could read, write, and draw beautifully – and he played a lively trumpet.

Then, one day, Samuel found a note on the kitchen table. It said, "We are getting very old and frail now, so we are going off on our very last big adventure. So Honeysuckle Cottage is yours now, Samuel dear. You have been like a son to us, and we will never forget you. So be happy and be good."

Samuel was not one to cry, but there was a tear in his eye as he read these words. The two people who were like his Ma and Pa had gone forever. Now he was alone.

In Honeysuckle Cottage there were lots of interesting things that the explorers had brought back from around the world. There were drums from Africa, carved elephants from India, and a shiny gong from Thailand. Perhaps it was time for him to have his own adventures, thought Samuel Bear. And what he wanted to do most was to learn about other bears.

He wanted to see why some lived by rivers, others in mountains, and why some preferred cold weather to hot. Then he could write a book about them, so that everyone would understand more about them and always treat them kindly. He could call the book *Bears of the World*.

That was a good idea! So he got out his atlas with lots of pictures of the world and maps. He took a pin, then shut his eyes and stuck the pin down on a page.

It landed on China – so that was it! Off he would go to China, where the panda bears lived. Panda bears were really different in that they only ate bamboo.

So he bought an aeroplane ticket. How exciting was that? He'd never been on a plane before, but the explorers had, and they told him all about it. So it wasn't long before, mission accomplished, he was deep in the bamboo forests of China, studying panda bears.

Panda bears are a secretive lot, but they didn't mind Samuel because he was a bear too. Already he had been busy with his sketch pad. There was a nice drawing of a panda cutting bamboo and another of a panda eating bamboo. But one mother panda always seemed to be cross, even though her cub was a very good one.

Then, in a clearing in the forest, he discovered that she was also looking after two young Teddy Bears. The only ones Samuel had ever seen before were stuffed toy teddies. But these were real, with golden curly fur!

"I found them hiding in the bamboo when they were just little scraps," Mother Panda explained. "But they are such a boisterous pair I've had to put them in a pen." She wrung her paws. "Din! Din!" she scolded, which means "behave yourself".

For a moment, Samuel could hardly believe his eyes. Then he remembered all the fun he'd had as a cub, building dens in Windy Wood, and suddenly he had a brilliant idea.

"Can I take them to live with me?" asked Samuel. "I have a cottage in England. There's plenty of room for all of us."

Mother Panda looked surprised, but Samuel's friendly face convinced her.

With an enormous grin, she opened the pen and the two Teddies scampered out. They sniffed Samuel's feet and tickled his toes. They played chase around his legs. A great big chuckle welled up in Samuel's tummy.

"Ha ha ha!" he chortled.

The little Teddies jumped up and down with glee. Nothing could stop them having fun. Samuel knew he would have his paws full if he took them home, but he didn't mind a bit!

"You're going back to Windy Wood with me," he told them. Now he would have a real family again.

So, with his backpack full of little leafy parcels of food wrapped up by Mother Panda, he hoisted the Teddies up, one on each shoulder. Then, waving goodbye, he set off through the bamboo forests on his way to the port.

3

Away to the Port

As he jogged along, Samuel sang the Teddies a song to keep them amused. And it went like this:

Beary weary beary bee,
Beary weary up a tree,
Beary weary wants to see
lots of lovely honey bees,
and get some lovely honey!

This made the Teddies even more wriggly.

However, once they reached the orange river and they had all settled on the bank, Samuel opened his backpack to look for snacks. But the Teddies had got there first.

"Deary me!" said Samuel, as he rummaged around his emergency supplies.

He studied their bright, furry faces.

"I'm going to open your eyes to a new world," he said. "But you're alike as pudding and pie! So that's what I will call you. Pudding and Pie it is. But which of you is which? Ha ha! I can't say right now. What fun we are going to have trying to tell you apart."

Then they were off again, over a creaking rope bridge, swinging this way and that, and with the Teddies shrieking and chortling. What fun they were having! Then, all of a sudden, there was an ominous sound, like something breaking. And it was!

CRACK! SNAP! BANG! went a big rope holding up the bridge. Desperately, Samuel clung on to the rope in front. Then he threw himself forward, as behind them the bridge disappeared down into the rushing river below.

"Phew! That was a narrow escape," he said, breathing a sigh of relief once they were safely on the other side.

Then they were away again, making their way down a windy mountain track.

Soon the port of Chin-chin came into view.

"Hurray!" shouted Samuel.

Soon Pudding and Pie's bright eyes were agog at all the busy sights and sounds. There were boats bobbing on the quay as sampans, junks, steamers, schooners and tankers all jostled to be loaded and unloaded.

"We are off to England," he told the man in the Customs House as he produced a crumpled passport.

"Very sorry, sir," said the Chinese man, eyeing up the Teddies. "More please!" He reached out a hand.

Samuel gave him a piece of paper with "SAMUEL BEAR, BRITISH BEAR EXPERT" written in big letters, but the Chinese man wasn't impressed.

"Very young bears only leave country for very special reasons," he said firmly. By now Pudding and Pie were fidgeting, and Samuel was getting worried. He couldn't leave the Teddy Bears behind now, could he?

So he hailed a rickshaw on the cobbled street, and after a rickety-rackety ride they arrived at a very large building. They hurried inside, where they were greeted by an ancient gentleman surveying piles of papers. It was the Ambassador.

"Teddy Bears!" he exclaimed when he saw Pudding and Pie, and his brown face cracked into a smile.

"They are orphans, said Samuel. "I found them in the forest." He told the Ambassador all about his work studying other bears.

"I am sure you will make an excellent guardian," said the Ambassador kindly. He gave Samuel a special letter stamped with a dragon. "Now you must have their photographs taken for the Record Office, and please let me have a copy of your book when it is published."

4

Over the Ocean Waves

"That's the boat for us!" exclaimed Samuel, when he saw a colourful junk called Sea-eye heave-hoeing at the port. It wasn't long before they were hurrying up the gangplank and settling into a nice cosy cabin.

There were two little hammocks for Pudding and Pie and a large bunk for

Samuel. Soon they were on their way, bouncing over the ocean waves. The Teddies' tummies were bouncing too!

"Oh dear," said Samuel, when Pudding and Pie were seasick all over the deck. But soon the Teddy Bears had found their sea-legs. They sniffed the salty air while Samuel sang lively sea shanties.

"Pull! Pull! Pull on the rope, you lubbers!" he bellowed, and Pudding and Pie heaved on the imaginary ropes. Then they played at being pirates, and Pudding and Pie hid in all sorts of strange places.

A sailor heard the Teddy Bears' names, and when Samuel wasn't looking he grabbed Pudding.

“I’m going to eat you because I like puddings,” he threatened.

Then he caught Pie.

“You’ll taste even better!” he said, smirking.

Pudding and Pie were all of a wobble when Samuel came back, but by now the horrid sailor had disappeared. Then Samuel spotted the flag tangled around the mast.

“If I was much younger, I would sort that out,” he said.

Quick as a wink, Pudding and Pie shinned up the mast as fast as their furry legs could carry them. Soon the jolly flag was flying free and dancing in the breeze again.

As they peered down, the Teddies could see for miles across the shiny ocean, and below them on deck stood Samuel Bear, waving and looking quite small!

Captain Skim was very pleased with Pudding and Pie for sorting out the flag.

"But what strange names for two clever Teddy Bears," he said.

So next day they were given new ones.

Captain Skim splashed Pudding's head with sea water and said, "I name you Laura," as instructed by Samuel. Then he splashed Pie's head too, while Samuel said, "I name you Lulu."

They were names Samuel liked the sound of, and now he could definitely tell them apart. Laura didn't rush into things like her sister Lulu.

The Teddy Bears were very happy with their nice new names. Now, no one would want to eat them.

To keep Laura and Lulu out of mischief, Samuel gave them daily lessons. There were lots of new words to learn, like "Stop", "Look", and "Listen."

The Teddy Bears were very bright, and if they didn't get it the first time, they got it the second. Soon they were copying every word that Samuel said, and making up some new ones too, chattering nineteen to the dozen.

But that didn't stop them getting up to mischief. One day Lulu pulled at some string sticking out from under a tarpaulin.

"Stop it!" squeaked a cross black rat. "You teddy bears are ruining my stowaway holiday, running about and frightening me half to death."

Lulu said she was sorry and gave the rat two hard ship's biscuits.

Next day they saw the poor rat thrashing about in the water.

"Save me! Save me!" it shouted.

Laura and Lulu tossed down a rope and the Rat struggled up.

"Thanks!" it grunted, before disappearing.

That evening they heard the nasty sailor say, "Thank goodness we've got rid of the pesky rat that's been pinching the ship's biscuits."

They were pleased to know they'd saved its life.

One day there was a "WHOOSH!" and a flock of strange geese landed on the deck. The geese were supposed to be flying over the Himalayas but had lost their way. One kept honking "South! South!" very loudly, so Samuel got out his compass and gave them some new directions.

Before they left one of the geese told Laura and Lulu some thrilling tales about giant snowballs that rolled across the ice and slippery frozen lakes they skidded on when taking off. It made the Teddies shiver with excitement inside their little furry coats.

Sleek dolphins often played around the boat too, having games of chase and somersaulting in the salt spray. Once they even saw a spouting whale sending a big plume of water high in the air. Sailing the ocean waves was definitely better than playing in a bamboo pen, and before long the ship's tailor had made them smart little sailor suits.

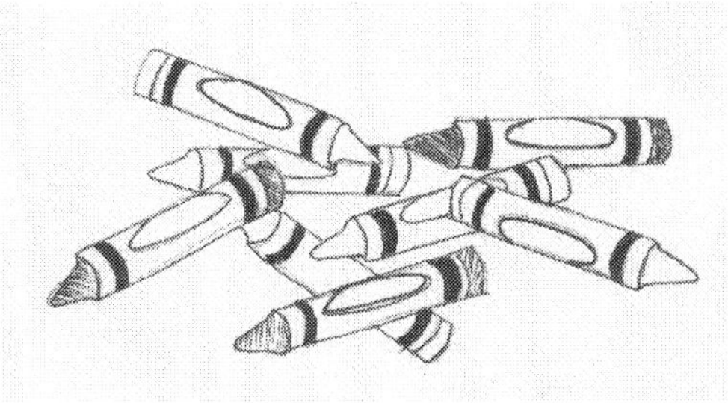

5

Windy Wood

Boats, buses and trains were all muddled up in the tired Teddies' heads when they arrived back at Uncle Samuel's home at Honeysuckle Cottage, Crab Apple Lane, Windy Wood.

"A good night's sleep is what you need," said Samuel. They scampered ahead up to the guest room under the eaves, where two little beds covered with patchwork covers were waiting. There were bear pictures on the walls too. But the Teddies weren't used to little beds. They piled up the bedclothes, put a pillow on the top, and slept on the little mountains. Samuel got a surprise when he came in next morning!

Soon they were down in the kitchen for breakfast while Samuel rummaged around in the cupboards for something nice to eat. There were crunchy nuts, wheatie flakes and tinned milk, all stored ready for his return. Then Samuel found two little bowls, and a big one too, and they all tucked in.

However, the Teddies had quite forgotten their manners. They banged on the table with their spoons and stuck their noses into the bowls. Worst of all, they licked their plates clean. But Samuel didn't mind a bit. It was great to have a new family.

Then they rushed out into the garden with Samuel padding behind. It was a tumble of weeds, and many trees were wearing pretty autumn colours. Lots of leaves had already fallen.

"This will make a lovely playground for young Teddy Bears," thought Samuel, as Lulu picked up pawfuls of leaves and tossed them into the air. Then Samuel fetched a rake from the garden shed and piled the leaves high. The Teddies dived in and scattered them everywhere again.

"It's fun to be young!" chortled Samuel, and he lowered his big furry body to the ground, tucked in his head, and did an enormous roly-poly. Before he was on his feet again, Laura and Lulu had scampered back into the cottage and were playing in the sitting-room, with its two big sofas, three armchairs, and lots of diamond-paned windows. Lulu jumped on the sofa and toppled a cushion. Then Laura toppled one too. Soon they were playing roly-poly over the cushions and roly-polying over each other on the floor too.

"Early days!" laughed Samuel.

He looked at the books in the bulging bookcases. What fun they would have!

Soon all three bears were climbing the twisty stairs to Samuel's studio, which was full of pots of paint, brushes and paper, and an over-worked easel. Samuel gave Laura and Lulu some coloured crayons and paper to play with. Then he pinned a panda picture on the easel.

While he was busy painting, Laura and Lulu were busy too. First, they rolled the crayons about. Then they drew round wobbly shapes: red ones, green ones, brown ones, and blue ones, all with stick legs.

Samuel knew they were trying to copy him, so he wrote 'Panda Bears' underneath. Then he found a piece of card and wrote 'Laura and Lulu' in big letters to pin over their bedroom door.

"Laura and Lulu," he said.

"Laura and Lulu," repeated the Teddy Bears, jumping up and down.

Suddenly the telephone rang, and Samuel dashed downstairs to answer it. When he came back there were splodges of paint all over the wall.

"Deary me!" said Uncle Samuel, very surprised. But he found a big paintbrush and made the brown splodges into tree trunks, the green splodges into leaves, and the ones that were red and blue into parrots. The Teddy Bears liked the lovely jungly picture.

6

The Village Shop

"We're off to the village today," said Samuel. "There's shopping to do."

It was a warm, sparkly sort of day, and soon they were off with Samuel carrying an enormous shopping bag. On the way, they stopped to pick some early blackberries. Samuel reached up to the big purply black ones on the high brambles. Then he cut a crooked stick so that he could pull them down. He cut a stick for Laura and Lulu too. That was fun. Soon their paws were all stained and juicy.

Oh dear, never mind, thought Samuel, as they licked them clean.

Suddenly, a surprised rabbit scampered off, its white tail bobbing, and Laura and Lulu shot off too.

"Not so fast," called Samuel, who was finding it difficult to keep up.

Once they reached the village, he made them stay close by his side.

They pressed their noses hard against Mrs Bennett's shop window, where jars of bright sweets stood in rows.

"Oh!" squealed Laura, who liked the pretty dolly mixtures best.

Inside, Mrs Bennett was busy serving. She stopped when she saw Samuel's smiling face.

"Did you have a good trip?" she asked, smiling back in welcome.

Then she spotted the two young Teddy Bears.

"Whatever have you got there?" she asked, a very surprised look on her face. She was used to mischievous children in her shop, but not young bears.

"Meet my new family," Samuel said proudly. "Laura and Lulu have come to live with me in Windy Wood."

"Oh, deary me," she exclaimed. "Won't you have your paws full?"

Meanwhile Laura was staring transfixed at Mrs Bennett, wondering what the swingy things were dangling from her ears. Mrs Bennett's earrings jangled backwards and forwards every time she moved her head.

Meanwhile, no one noticed that Lulu had disappeared. Suddenly, a head popped up on the other side of the counter, right next to Mrs Bennett, a furry paw reached out, and a bar of chocolate disappeared from a box.

“My, oh my,” said Mrs Bennett. “You can’t do that, my dear. Even Teddy Bears have to behave.”

Samuel fetched Lulu and held her paw tightly.

“No, Lulu, Teddy Bears mustn’t run round the counter,” he said firmly.

“You’ll be needing some reins,” snapped Mrs Stringer, who was waiting to be served.

“They’ve only just arrived from China, so everything is new to them,” said Samuel. “But they are very bright young Teddy Bears. They will soon learn.”

Samuel chose some groceries from the shelves and Mrs Bennett packed them into a bag.

"And two candy sticks please," he added, pressing a shiny coin into a paw of each of the Teddies to pay for them. Soon Lulu and Laura were busy eating the sticky treats. and words like 'little darlings' and 'angels' sailed over their heads.

Next they all went off to the Post Office, where Samuel bought a little book of stamps and some envelopes. Mr Amos the postmaster gave both Laura and Lulu some stickers and a book to put them in.

The sun was shining brightly when the bears left the Post Office, and then it was off to the park where there were swings, a roundabout, and a slide.

"Hold tight," said Samuel when they both jumped on the roundabout.

"Up in the air and down again," he sang when it was time for the swings.

Then a little girl arrived.

"Look, Mummy, Teddy Bears on the swings!"

Lulu pointed at the slide.

Samuel steered the wobbly swings to a halt.

"Wait until it really stops before you get off," he told them.

The Teddy Bears liked the big blue slide best. They whooshed down it fast.

All too soon it was time to go.

"We must get home in time for lessons," said Samuel, firmly.

7

Paw Prints

Samuel was writing about bears' feet for his book, so he thought paw printing would be a good idea. Laura and Lulu had shown him how much they liked paint. They had a lovely wall picture to prove it! So Samuel mixed some bright coloured paint for them to use. The Teddies watched closely.

"You'll know how to do this next time," he said. "Now, dip a paw in the paint and press it hard on the paper!"

It was such fun that soon they'd made several smudgy paw prints, all going in different directions. Then they made a row that looked all the same.

"That's a good one," said Samuel to Laura, when he spotted a special picture with no drips or splashes. It was perfect! "Can you do one like that?" he asked Lulu.

Of course she could. She couldn't let Laura beat her!

"When the paint is dry, you can cut the paw prints out," Samuel promised.

Then they looked at the paws section of Samuel's book. There was a polar bear standing on the ice, looking very big and fierce. Next to a small square with a picture of a paw with great big claws.

The Teddies looked at their own. Their claws were tiny and their paws had soft pads.

"We can send some of your paw prints with a letter to the Ambassador in China," said Samuel. "I'm sure he will like that."

Laura and Lulu were still practising hard at writing their names. Some of the letters were quite spidery. Making a paw print was easier.

Soon the Teddy Bears were discovering how easy it was to cut in the wrong place when they tried to use scissors.

“Practice makes perfect,” said Samuel, as he snipped carefully away.

Suddenly there was a knock at the door. It was Mrs Bennett’s daughter, Rosie. She had brought a basket of groceries.

“With Mum’s compliments,” Rosie said, grinning as she spotted the Teddies’ handiwork. “You’re a good teacher, Mr Samuel. We do things like that at school. You can make some of those prints into wallpaper.”

“Feet would be quicker,” Samuel decided.

He helped the Teddies walk about on the paper. Soon the kitchen floor was awash with sheets of wet paw prints, and suddenly Samuel slipped and plonked himself down in the middle of one sheet.

"I don't think bottom prints are a good idea!" he laughed, rubbing his sore bottom. The Teddies tried to stifle their giggles.

Rosie set up the clothes airer and hung the printed sheets up to dry.

Next Samuel fetched the photo album. Inside were pictures of him as a cub. He did look funny in his baby clothes! There was a photo of him playing in a sand pit and another at the seaside.

Rosie chuckled. "Weren't you cute, Mr Bear, when you were small?"

"That reminds me," said Samuel. "We could send a nice photograph of you two Teddies to the Chinese Ambassador. Then he can see how much you've grown! "

Laura held her paw above Lulu's head.

"Growing," said Samuel. "You are getting bigger."

Then Lulu held her paw over Laura's.

"Lulu big," she said, grinning.

Then Lulu held her paw over Laura's head.

"Laura big too," said Lulu, jumping up and down.

Samuel gave a big grin.

"We must put up a wall chart, then you can measure yourselves every day," he said brightly. "Now I'll see whether the playhouse is still in the loft!"

Samuel was so excited at his mission that he didn't even stop to unpack the chocolate biscuits Rosie had brought.

8

What Shall We Do Today?

Samuel was making plans. He was always making plans now. Really, it was great to have a family again. There were lots of things for Laura and Lulu to find out. There were puzzles, games and sum cards to do.

They collected conkers in the wood under the horse chestnut tree to use for counting, and soon they knew how many conkers make five. Then they found acorns under the oak tree and weighed them with the scales. They played snap with animal picture cards and looked at lots of story books too.

Samuel found boxes to make shakers and filled them with rice to make music. The Teddies loved them, clapping their paws while Samuel sang fun songs. Then they listened to Samuel playing his trumpet.

But one day Samuel was finishing a picture he was painting when a loud "GONG-ONG-ONG!" shook the cottage.

CRASH! went the paint.

Samuel closed his eyes and made a wish. With lessons to squeeze in, his book to finish and everything else to do, what he needed was another pair of hands.

So he made out a card saying: 'Mr Samuel Bear requires help urgently. Please apply to: Honeysuckle Cottage, Crab Apple Lane, Windy Wood.' Then he put it in Mrs Bennett's shop window.

Soon a letter arrived from a Mrs Scrub. Samuel arranged a visit.

On Tuesday Mrs Scrub bustled in, carrying a bulging shopping bag and with her hair tied up in a duster.

"I can cook, I can clean, and I've never 'ad any complaints!" she said proudly.

Then she spotted Laura and Lulu sitting quietly on the sofa, sharing a picture book. Their golden fur was glistening from a good brushing.

"I never realized you 'ad young 'uns!" she grumbled, her tone changing. "But I must say they look like little angels!"

Samuel nodded and smiled proudly. "They are being properly brought up."

"If the pay is good, then I'll be 'appy to 'elp," said Mrs Scrub.

Then a bee buzzed in from the garden. Samuel watched its mad flight around the room. After hovering over Lulu, it settled on her nose. It must have smelt the honey that she'd forgotten to lick off.

Lulu struck out with a paw and caught her sister's ear.

"Buzz buzz buzz," went the bee.

"Ouch!" said Laura, tumbling off the sofa, and the picture book sailed through the air. It hit the bowl of fresh roses gathered for the occasion, sending petals and water splattering everywhere. The Teddy Bears looked like escapees from a wedding! Soon there was pandemonium as the pair chased each other round the room, Lulu after the bee and Laura after Lulu.

"Angels indeed! I'd call them little devils," said Mrs Scrub.

She marched towards the door. "A lucky escape I've 'ad!" she muttered. "Youngsters – you can keep 'em!"

As she closed the door behind her, Laura and Lulu crash-landed in a pile on the floor giggling, just as the bee was making its escape. They looked at Uncle Samuel who stood rooted to the spot.

Suddenly a huge grin spread across his whiskery face.

"Mrs Scrub wouldn't have suited us," he chuckled. "She was too fussy! Now off you go and wash, or I'll get out the hosepipe."

For now, he would have to manage on his own.

9

Gardening Time

"Ho ho ho! Hee hee! Gardening is the job for me!" sang Samuel at breakfast next day. He wanted to keep the Teddies busy, and he hoped his new rhyme would make them want to do some gardening.

The sun was shining brightly, sending bright patterns through the window. There couldn't be a better time to introduce the Teddies to gardening. He had already cleared two little patches of earth, one for each of them.

Once they had finished breakfast, he cleared the table and got out an old cardboard box. It was full of seeds that the explorers had gathered on their travels. Inside there were big stripy seeds, squiggly little ones, very wrinkly ones, and nice smooth ones. But they weren't in packets, so he would get the Teddies to sort them. Wouldn't it be fun if any of them would grow?

Samuel spread a sheet of paper on the table and tipped out the seeds. Lulu made a pile of the stripy ones and the wrinkly ones. Laura chose to sort the squiggly little ones and the nice smooth ones. Then Samuel talked to them about tools.

He gave them two little trowels and two little hand forks.

Then they were off. Outside. Ready.

Once the Teddies had planted the seeds, they watered them. And watered them. And watered them.

Lulu thought it was fun to water Laura too! Then Laura chased after Lulu, because it was her turn to do the same. All good fun! But they couldn't catch Samuel, he ran too fast.

At bedtime, Laura and Lulu went to their bedroom window and looked out. They were hoping to see some plants already growing, like Jack's beanstalk that Uncle Samuel had told them about.

"A watched seed never grows," Samuel said when he came to tuck them into bed. "You see, some seeds germinate quickly and others take longer. We'll just have to wait and see what comes up first."

Then he had a thought.

"I know what we'll do. We'll sow some mustard and cress."

Next morning he fetched two little dishes and some kitchen paper. Then he found a packet of mustard seed and one of cress that had come with a gardening magazine. Wasn't that lucky?

Once they had covered the dishes with paper and wetted it thoroughly, Lulu scattered the mustard seeds on her dish, and Laura sowed the cress seeds on hers. Then Samuel put the saucers on the windowsill so they would get plenty of light to help them to grow.

A couple of days later the little seeds had split open and little shoots had begun to appear. Every day, Laura and Lulu watched the shoots carefully to see if they were growing, and Samuel was pleased he could get on with writing his book.

After a few more days, Samuel said it was time to cut the little plants with scissors. The teddies made sandwiches by spreading their mustard and cress on bread and butter ready for tea-time. Wasn't that good? Laura and Lulu really enjoyed eating them because they were special.

And guess what? A few days later they looked out the window and a big patch of rainbow bright flowers had sprung up.

"I think those seeds must have come all the way from Africa," said Samuel. "You see, when the rains come after a long dry spell, all the flowers come out at once."

Just like that!

Growing things was exciting, decided the Teddies.

10

Story Magic

When Uncle Samuel reached down the big fairy story book from the shelf, Laura and Lulu jumped up and down with glee. It was the one with the wrinkled corners that Uncle Samuel had loved as a cub. Then, with Laura and Lulu sitting comfortably on the floor, he settled himself in the armchair to read to them.

"Once upon a time," he began in his best story-telling voice. It made their little hearts beat even faster, for soon they would be in the land of make-believe where anything could happen! There was a wicked queen who tricked Snow White into eating a poisoned apple. There was a giant too, who climbed a beanstalk growing so high that it reached the sky! But the story the Teddies liked best was about Hansel and Gretel, the two little children who got lost in the woods. There was a lovely picture in the book too.

At first Samuel wouldn't read that story because it might remind them of things best forgotten. But in the end he gave in, for the sake of some peace and quiet. Then one day Laura said, "Let's be Hansel and Gretel! There are lots of woods to hide in. But we won't use crumbs, because we know the birds will eat them."

So the Teddies practised trailing pebbles round the trees at the end of the garden, but pebbles were heavy to carry.

Suddenly Laura had a brilliant idea.

"We could use paper instead," she said. "There's stacks of old newspapers in the garden shed."

Soon they were tearing them into little pieces until they had a bag full.

"I'll lay the trail," announced Lulu. "But give me plenty of time to hide."

Then she was off.

Laura closed her eyes and counted. She counted up to ten. But when she got to twenty, she got in a muddle and had to start again. Then for good measure she said her ABC too.

"Ready!" she said, and she set off with Uncle Samuel to find Lulu. This was the fun part – finding Lulu.

Meanwhile, in the wood, Lulu had skipped among the trees, showering little clouds of paper behind her. Then she went through the gaps between the bushes. Once she tiptoed over the stepping-stones across a little stream and threw a shower of paper the other side. She could see the trail winding out behind her.

She was so busy that she didn't notice the crows and rooks cawing in the trees above. They had pecked the fields bare. Now they had settled in the wood. Soon a nosy crow flew down cawing: "Food-or-not! Food-or-not!" It pecked away at the trail of paper. Others quickly followed, and soon a patch had completely disappeared.

Once the bag was empty, Lulu climbed a tree. On a comfy branch she sat to wait with an excited feeling in her tum.

She waited and waited. Her tummy felt empty, and the sky began to grow dark. Fierce tears scalded her cheeks. Where was Laura? Where was Uncle

Sam? She didn't feel happy or excited anymore.

"Boo-hoo," she cried, with a tingle of fear and disappointment. She disturbed an owl on the branch above.

"OO-OO-OO!" it hooted, then left in a flurry of wings.

Exhausted, Lulu fell asleep.

Suddenly there was a crunching of twigs, and a torch flashed. It was Uncle Sam and Laura!

Uncle Sam opened his arms wide, and a tearful Lulu climbed down.

"Creepy crawlies must have eaten the paper," Laura said quietly.

"Never mind, you're safe now," said Samuel, and he gave Lulu a great big bear hug.

"You've had an adventure, like me," he said.

Back in the cottage Samuel made the Teddies hot chocolate, and they munched raspberry buns.

"Lucky I found you before you got Too-hoo-hoo lonely!" he chuckled. And the Teddy Bears giggled their socks off!

11

The Book Shop

Uncle Samuel had promised to take Laura and Lulu to town as a treat to buy a book. His own bearhood books were very special, but the Teddies needed to choose their own. And there were lots to choose from at Bookstop, his favourite shop.

They sped along in the bus, passing High Hill, where Samuel liked to picnic, and fair Meadows Park, where there were lots of frolicking deer. Samuel thought happily of the lovely big house there with lots of rooms that he loved to wander through on open days. It would be a summer treat for the Teddies.

Soon they'd arrived at the little town of Happyville, and once inside the shop doorway, a funny clown picture on a book cover caught Laura's eye. Uncle Samuel reached it down, and she was soon engrossed. The clowns were juggling, riding unicycles and balancing baskets and doing all sorts of tricks. Laura was hooked. She clutched the book tightly – she didn't want to lose it!

But Lulu was soon rushing through the piles of glossy books, one after the other.

"Hey, slow down!" said Uncle Sam. "Or you will tear the pages."

The shop lady kept tut-tutting at Uncle Samuel and the Teddy Bears. It was all well and good to have the custom of bears, but they still had to be careful. It was all too exciting for Lulu.

She eventually calmed down when she found a pop-up book on science with lots of fun experiments in, showing little volcanoes exploding and torches with flashing lights. Then she sat, carefully opening it and closing it to see the bottles and flasks spring to life, while Samuel wandered off to study some books on the high shelves, though still keeping a watchful eye open for the Teddies.

He wanted to see what bear books were coming out at present that might steal his thunder, and he soon found one with a bear on the cover catching fish. That was what he wanted to do most, go somewhere like Canada where there were plenty of fish in the rivers. Now he would have to wait for the Teddies to get a bit older, and then they could all go. What fun that would be, camping out by the rivers and lakes!

Finally, Samuel found a book about climbing mountains. Just the job! Climbing mountains could be very dangerous, even for a bear.

By this time Lulu was sitting cross-legged on the floor, sharing a book with Laura. This time it was about knights and dragons, and several children had gathered round to watch. Lulu was turning the pages very carefully.

12

All the Fun of the Fair

It wasn't long before Samuel had told his friend Mrs Bennett about his problems – how hard it was to be a good uncle and a successful author all at the same time. Really, he wasn't getting much of his book done, and could do with some help.

Mrs Bennett suggested that Rosie, her daughter, would love to help.

"Rosie's a big girl now, and quite capable," she said.

Samuel was overjoyed. He would still have time for lessons, and once his book was done, time for fun too.

"Rosie is going to take you to the fair while I get some typing done," Samuel told the excited Teddies one morning.

It sounded a wonderful idea. They'd seen lorries unloading brightly painted sideshows and rides in a field near the village, and Samuel had told them all about the fun of the fair. If they stood on a stump near Samuel's cottage, they could hear music and shouts of laughter. It was an exciting noise.

Then the great day came. Soon the Teddy Bears were discovering just how exciting it really was. There were balls to throw at coconuts on sticks. There were galloping painted horses to ride that whirled round and round. There were pennies to roll down and topple other piles, and toys to fish for with a grabbing arm. Rosie managed to hook a purse for her mother.

Then it was time for the ghost train.

"I hope you like being scared," said Rosie happily.

Lulu wasn't sure, not after her adventure in the wood, though she certainly wouldn't say so. In they climbed, and the train chugged away into a dark tunnel.

Suddenly a flapping thing frightened them half to death! OOOOO-

OOOOOO! went a scary ghost, and a big cobweb dropped on Laura's head. They all grabbed each other tightly. Lulu was glad it wasn't on her head. Even Rosie was scared. They squeaked and squealed all through the windy tunnels that twisted this way and that, swaying as they went.

Up above, big black bats hovered at every corner, and enormous witches' cats with flashing yellow eyes purred loudly, while every now and then a scary skeleton appeared. Suddenly they were chugging out again into broad daylight. Then everything was alright again.

It wasn't long before they were zooming up and down on a rollercoaster, so fast that it took their breath away.

Then Rosie said, "We have only got enough money left for one more ride or game."

The Teddies' smiles disappeared.

"Oh well, we'll have one ride on the dodgems," said Rosie. "We can bash the other cars, but keep your paws tucked in."

A red car with the number 10 on the side came to a halt and they climbed in. Then Rosie put her foot on the pedal and they shot off. At first, they were spinning round and round, and everyone rammed them hard. They were all jolted this way and that, then Rosie looked fierce and said, "Hang on tight!" She drove round fast, dodging the other cars as Laura and Lulu shrieked loudly.

Suddenly the fair owner spotted them.

"Celebrity bears!" he said. "We've never had teddy bears at our fair before, and now everyone will want to come to see them."

He gave them lots of tokens for free rides and games, so they were able to whirl round and round in the big wheel high over people's heads, until they almost felt sick. Then they played lots of bingo games, because it was fun matching numbers on the card with Rosie. Eventually they won a new watch for Uncle Samuel, and a big stripy tie too. Wouldn't he be pleased?

But they all had to agree there was nothing quite so super to eat as whirly-

whirly wisps of sugary candy-floss that they watched being spun from a spinning drum.

Oh, what a fun day it had been.

13

Cooking with Rosie

In his studio Samuel Beresford Bear, artist and writer, was very happy, because he'd just had a call from his agent wanting to know how his bear book was coming on, and could he come up to London for a chat? Yes, of course he could – he had Rosie to look after the Teddies. He could also warn his agent that there might be some delay in finishing the book now he was bringing up two young Teddies.

Down in the kitchen he could hear the clash and batter of the Teddy Bears cooking with her. It gave him a good feeling in his tum, because they were making Christmas goodies in plenty of time for Christmas. There would be potted mincemeat, a nice plum pudding – and, of course, the cake.

They were starting with the cake because it would get richer and fruitier with keeping. Laura and Lulu were helping Rosie spread everything on the table. It made a wonderful sight.

The Teddies had never seen so many interesting things before, and they found it difficult to keep their paws off.

"Now, now," said Rosie. "You've got to behave. Uncle Samuel is relying on you to be good."

The Teddy Bears were wearing plastic aprons, early Christmas presents from Mrs Bennett, and on the front were pictures of Father Christmas and the elves.

"Flour," said Rosie loudly. "We have to start with flour if we are making a cake." She took some big spoonfuls out of the bag and dropped them through a sieve. A white dust filled the air as the Teddies watched excitedly. They both wished they could have done that.

Then Rosie cut up chunks of butter and dolloped those into another bowl. Laura and Lulu were wondering when they would get their chance to do something when Rosie said, "You can grate the peel off this orange, but watch your paws."

Next minute Laura was pushing the orange up and down to make a little pile of squiggly pieces on the plate.

"That's called zest," said Rosie. "It gives the cake a nice flavour."

Lulu was bouncing up and down too, itching to start. Then she was given eggs to crack open and drop into the bowl and beat up. It was lovely fun.

Rosie was enjoying herself too. It was great being in charge. Her mum always said that cooking was a chore, but she couldn't agree.

The house hummed with activity. Samuel was busy upstairs, Rosie and the Teddies were busy downstairs, and outside in the garden the birds were busy too. The Teddy Bears had hung up little treats for them. There was a string bag of peanuts and handfuls of bird seed on the wooden bird table.

"Cuckoo! Cuckoo!" chimed the clock in the kitchen. By now the rich mixture was complete, and the Teddies looked up to see the little cuckoo pop in and out of the clock.

"Let me see if the oven is hot," said Rosie, and she went over to check if the signal light had come on.

"Yes, it is," she said, giggling gleefully. Then they took turns dolloping the mixture into the greased tin.

"We'll pop it in, and then we'll call Uncle Samuel," she said. "He will be glad of a break."

Then Rosie carried the tin aloft, like a beautifully jewelled crown, across the room to the oven.

"We must time it," she said, glancing at the clock. "It's just after 11 o'clock now, so the cake should be ready by two."

Then Laura and Lulu rushed to the bottom of the stairs.

"Uncle Sam, Uncle Sam, we've finished!" they called.

Uncle Sam came thudding down the stairs.

"The book is coming along nicely," he grinned. "But I can't smell anything yet."

He sniffed the air.

"Well, it's just gone in the oven," said Laura.

Suddenly Samuel spotted the big bowl on the table. There were lots of rich scrapings around the sides, and he couldn't resist dipping his paw in. Next minute he was sucking on it loudly.

"Oh, you are a one!" said Rosie. "That won't teach the young Bears to behave."

Samuel grinned.

"But it will save on the washing up," he joked.

Next minute Laura and Lulu had joined in too.

"Cooked, it will be even better!" exclaimed Samuel.

Already there was a draft of sweetness coming from the oven.

"Poor old pandas," said Samuel. "They've got to make do with bamboo!"

14

A Christmas Surprise

The day had arrived, and Uncle Samuel had gone to London to see his publisher and find out what he had to do to get his book just right. Rosie was in charge of the Teddies and had decided to take Laura and Lulu into Happyville for a treat to see all the Christmas decorations.

Now they were peering at a toy shop window because Rosie had lost her purse and had gone back to find it. They could see in the corner of the shop window several Teddy Bears all dolled up with tinsel for Christmas, and all wearing bland smiles. That is, all except one, and Lulu spotted it first. It was looking quite cross and twitching its nose because a fly had landed on it.

"I'm sure that one moved," she said as they stared at the window.

Slowly the scruffy bear lifted its paw into the air and gave a sort of wave.

"There, he's alive and wants help," Lulu exclaimed. "Can't you see? We've spotted a real one instead of a lot of dummies!"

"But he's only just alive," added Laura, who on closer inspection noticed that Scruffy Bear was struggling to grin.

"Well, we'll have to rescue him," Lulu said emphatically. "We can't leave him there. He's one of us."

"But we can't buy him – just look at the price." Lulu pointed to the square label that clearly said £5. For a moment the Teddies looked unhappily at the floor.

"I know, let's kidnap him," said Lulu. "Look, his ear twitched!"

All the other bears with their smart bow ties and tartan pants looked very solid and stuffy, completely unaware of the drama.

"We'll have to think of something!" Laura declared. "What if he's sold?"

She signalled to the scruffy bear to keep still. Then she got some paper from her bag and wrote 'TRUST US!' in capital letters. She would have preferred to write 'HELP IS AT HAND' but the paper was too small.

"I hope he can read," said Laura, as Lulu held it high. The scruffy bear blinked, then he flopped back behind the others.

"Well, he has got a brain," Laura exclaimed, as she gave him a friendly wave.

"We could pretend we're customers and shout 'FIRE!'" suggested Lulu.

"Then, if everybody runs, we could grab him."

There was still no sign of Rosie.

"He looks tired and heavy," said Laura, worriedly. "Perhaps we need some help. Let's get a supermarket basket from Stuffbury's next door to carry him in."

"Great idea!" confirmed Lulu.

"If I had £5, I would buy a bear," she said loudly as they rushed off.

There were no baskets outside Stuffbury's, so they hurried down the first aisle, past rows of Christmas puddings, to find one. Suddenly Lulu felt like a ship that had struck a rock. A cheeky-faced youngster had struck her broadside with a trolley. She fell backwards and two solid Christmas puddings toppled onto her head.

Lulu struck out in a wild kind of war dance, uttering a moaning chant.

The child's mother quickly intervened.

"Say you're sorry, Petal," she said, unsure of what a cross bear might do.

"Shan't!" screamed Petal, lashing the side of the trolley with her foot.

Laura winced with imagined pain.

"She's a cross-patch today because I won't let her have another lolly," her mother explained to the Teddies. "She's had six already, and I don't want her to be sick."

"Quick, let's go," said Laura. "We don't want to skid on any sick."

Luckily a basket lay nearby so they grabbed it and ran. But when they got back to the toy shop, the scruffy bear had disappeared from the window. Lulu paled, and Laura's tummy did a roll.

The shop was very crowded. Several children were gathered around a huge Lego dinosaur towering in the centre, and there were grown-ups everywhere peering into boxes and fiddling with things, trying to make them work.

"Perhaps he's been sold," said Lulu, with a prickle in her eye.

Then Laura spotted him. He was being tidied up on the counter. He was on his back with his legs in the air, and beside him was a piece of shiny wrapping paper.

"It's now or never!" said Lulu, and she swung her basket at the Lego monster. It toppled sideways, bits hurtled through the air, and confusion reigned. Shop assistants went down and grovelled on their hands and knees to pick up the pieces.

Quick as a wink, Laura and Lulu grabbed Scruffy Bear and stuffed him in the basket, covering him with the sheet of shiny paper.

"The door!" piped up Laura as they rushed towards it.

"And we didn't have to shout 'FIRE!' puffed Lulu.

Suddenly Laura felt uncomfortably hot, realizing what they were about to do.

"Don't worry, he was worth it!" gasped Lulu, as they hurried round the corner.

Luckily, there was Rosie!

"Where have you been?" she asked. "I've been looking for you everywhere! And what have you here?"

Just then Scruffy Bear poked his head up, relieved that he wouldn't be stuffed down a Christmas stocking after all.

"Well, you can't put him back," said Rosie after she heard the story. "But we haven't enough money to pay for him either."

Back at the cottage they found a letter lying on the mat with a Chinese stamp on it.

"It's addressed to the Teddy Bears at Honeysuckle Cottage," said Rosie, picking it up.

"Oh, goody," chuckled Lulu. She couldn't wait to open it. Inside was a card shaped like a lantern from the Chinese ambassador, with a five-pound note in it.

"I said I would buy a bear," Lulu grinned happily. "Now we really can!"

"But we will have to post the money to the shop if we don't want to get into trouble," said Laura.

Suddenly Scruffy Bear sat up and looked about him.

"Thanks," he whispered.

"You're safe with us, brother bear," smiled Laura.

"Won't Uncle Samuel have a big surprise when he comes home tomorrow?" beamed Rosie.

"It will be our Christmas surprise," said Lulu.

Laura and Lulu bounced up and down with glee. They couldn't wait to see Uncle Samuel's face!

A Note from the Author

A big thank you to my publisher Debbie Young, to my editor Dan Gooding, and to my very first readers, Sophie and Louise. I hope you enjoy reading about the adventures of Samuel Bear and the Teddies as much as I enjoyed writing about them.

Betty x

Also by Betty Salthouse

ANIMAL ADVENTURES AT RAINBOW COTTAGE

Join Sidney Spider, Sarah Slug, William Woodlouse, Lucy Ladybird and their friends in Mrs Green's garden at Rainbow Cottage, where they live and play together and share exciting new experiences. Will Martin Millipede ever learn to count his legs?

Also by Betty Salthouse

MOTHER KOALA KNOWS BEST

AND OTHER AUSTRALIAN ANIMAL STORIES

This charming collection of short animal stories will be greatly enjoyed by any children who love native Australian wildlife. Beautiful illustrations by Pip Westgate bring the animals to life, including not only the more familiar koalas, kangaroos and wombats but also the lesser-known creatures, such as numbats, lyre birds and lorikeets.

Also by Betty Salthouse

CUCKOO CALL

Brains, the baby blackbird, thinks there's something odd about the huge new chick in the nest, but no-one else believes him. Can he save his family from disaster before it's too late? With the help of his new friend, Pij, the woodpigeon, he's determined to do his best.

This dramatic story about the survival of birds in the wild will appeal to any children who enjoy realistic stories about animals.

Also by Betty Salthouse

THE FOSSIL HUNTERS

When ten-year-old Jamie Rollings takes up fossil-hunting for a hobby, he stumbles across some exciting discoveries on the nearby estate that lead to new friendships and surprises that make this summer holiday truly special and unforgettable.

This traditional children's adventure story is set in an English country village in the days when children played outdoors with their friends all summer long. They seek their own entertainment and excitement in the real world instead of online, and the latest technology they have at their disposal is the fax machine!

Also by Betty Salthouse

PARROT TALK

When nine-year-old Jamie Horton rescues a lost parrot and smuggles it into his bedroom, he has to act fast to learn how to care for it without revealing his secret to his bossy big sister and anxious mum. But then the bird escapes and Jamie fears the worst.

Will Jamie ever see Sidney again? One thing's for certain – Jamie's life will never be the same again.

A traditional English adventure story, ideal for children who love animals, especially parrots and birdlife.

Printed in Great Britain
by Amazon

70413111R00064